Embracing the Call

PALMETTO
PUBLISHING
Charleston, SC
www.PalmettoPublishing.com

© 2024 by Elizabeth Figueroa

All rights reserved.
This book or any portion thereof may not be reproduced or used in any manner whatsoever without the express written permission of the publisher except for the use of brief quotations in a book review.

Paperback ISBN: 9798822966017

Embracing the Call

A WOMAN PASTOR

Elizabeth Figueroa

Contents

Introduction	1
Lesson #1: **Trust God Enough to Move in Obedience**	3
Lesson #2: **Obedience Unlocks Favor**	6
Lesson #3: **Move With or Without Support**	9
Lesson #4: **You Are Responsible to Fulfill the Vision**	11
Lesson #5: **Present Doesn't Always Mean Present**	13
Lesson #6: **The Leech Syndrome**	15
Lesson #7: **Nip It in the Bud**	18
Lesson #8: **Be Gracefully Firm**	21
Lesson #9: **Show Grace**	24
Lesson #10: **I'm Not Your Competition**	26
Lesson #11: **You Cannot Want It More Than Them**	29
Lesson #12: **Lonely Stroll**	32
Lesson #13: **Do Not Take It Personally**	35
Lesson #14: **To Invest or to Divest**	38
Lesson #15: **A Woman Pastor**	41

Dedication

To God
The glory belongs to You! It has always been and always will be about You. Thank You for Your faithfulness even when I did not deserve it. I love You, God!

To my Family
Thank you for always being my number one supporters! After God, you all are the reason why I strive daily to be better. I love you all dearly!

To my Fiancé
Miguel, God knew exactly what He was doing when He brought you into my life. Thank you for constantly pushing me to pursue all that God has promised and for genuinely loving me. I love you, sweetheart!

To my Pastor
Pastor Kenny, after God, I owe who I am today to you. From day one, you saw in me what I could not see in myself. Thank you for all the lessons along the way. You promised to always be there, and you have not failed me yet.

To Hope Restored Church
HRC Family, I could not have done this without you! Thank you for always believing in me, constantly supporting me, and fervently praying for me. It is truly an honor and a privilege to be your Pastor.

Introduction

My name is Elizabeth Figueroa, but I am better known as "Lisy." I was born and raised in Lancaster, PA, where I still reside today. I have two amazing children and am also recently engaged to the love of my life. I am the proud Pastor of Hope Restored Church. It still sounds surreal to introduce myself as such, but I love what I do! As someone who was not raised in church, I would have never thought that one day this would be my story. Truly, God works in mysterious ways. Prior to becoming a Pastor, I was in ministry as an Evangelist for about five years. I also had the blessing to work alongside my Pastor for thirteen years, which taught me many invaluable lessons. I had the privilege of serving as a Bible School Teacher, Worship Leader, Children's Ministry Director, Youth Pastor, Interpreter, and General Secretary of the church council throughout that time. Each of these roles has equipped me greatly for my role today as a Pastor. I began Hope Restored Church in July of 2022 with only four families. We have grown significantly since then and have had the opportunity to be a blessing to our community. Hope Restored Church is a place that embraces people and meets them where they are in their journey. We truly are a family. Our mission and vision has always focused on restoring hope to everyone who enters and discipling men and women to work for the Kingdom of God and pursue their calling. Though the calling over my life has come with many learning curves, I am passionate about serving God and His people. This is why I chose to share with you some life and spiritual lessons that I have learned along the way.

Lesson #1:
Trust God Enough to Move in Obedience

Trust in the LORD with all your heart, and do not rely on your own understanding; think about Him in all your ways, and He will guide you on the right paths.
—*Proverbs 3:5–6 (HCSB)*

Obedience can be a scary thing at times. It is such a simple concept and yet often so difficult to walk in. We tend to deem it a children's topic. Our children are taught the importance of being obedient. The irony is that we instill in them the importance of being obedient at all times, yet we greatly struggle with that same idea before our Heavenly Father. Whether the culprit is fear of failure, or desperation arising from uncertainty, or perhaps worry about what others will think or say, the truth is that obedience is always worth it!

For years, the Lord had spoken to me about a pastoral calling. I had my mind made up as to what that would look like. My husband and I would be in a stable and healthy marriage, my family would be complete with my children and all, and we would be faithfully walking in the will of the Lord. We would be ready to take on the task and hit the ground running. Sounds good, doesn't it? And yet none of this was the case. See, God's voice began to trickle in more and more throughout my intimacy with Him. The stronger His voice became, the more it penetrated my heart, and I simply knew the time was near to become a Pastor. The question was, would I trust God enough to move in obedience?

I began to ask the Lord to confirm things publicly if it truly was His timing. I began to receive confirmation after confirmation to the point that I could no longer fight against the current. What now? I wanted to move in obedience, but how? What did that even look like? I was a young, single woman who was still awaiting the promise of her children coming back home after losing custody of them years prior. How could I shepherd anyone? Nothing in my life was ordinary! Nothing in my walk with God was normal in the eyes of society. My idea of what a pastor's life looked like was nothing like my own. They were people who were married, older in age, had years of seminary under their belt, and had established careers and families. And yet I chose to trust the Lord and walk in total obedience to His voice. I trusted that He would provide just as He promised, and I understood that as long as I moved in obedience, I would become His responsibility. So I decided it was time to take a leap of faith and embrace the call.

Trusting God is not always the easiest of tasks. And yet the very reason that we wrestle with it is because it does not always make sense—not to the human mind, anyway. We want to lean on our own understanding because, after all, it is most logical. However, we must break out of the mentality that we serve a God who will limit Himself to moving in logical ways just to accommodate our finite minds. When we choose to acknowledge Him in all that we do, He graciously leads the way and guides us on the right path.

Sometimes trusting God enough to move in obedience comes at the cost of your reputation. Other times, simply put, it will put you in a position to look like you have lost your mind in the eyes of others. And yet none of this stopped Noah from building the ark, or Abraham from binding his son on the altar, or the woman with the issue of blood from making her way to Jesus. It could cost you relationships, careers, and many other things that you have worked so hard to achieve. It requires you to walk into the absolute unknown, to walk by faith without a clue of what awaits you, and to deposit your total trust in the One who called you.

Walking into the unknown is one of the scariest positions to put yourself in. You can be riddled with uncertainty and bombarded with hypothetical scenarios of things simply not working out. And yet this is exactly where trust comes in. Our Father expects us to trust Him with everything and in everything. Scripture is clear that we are not to lean on our own understanding. Doing so will limit us once fear and doubt set in, hence we so desperately need His guidance. After all, who better than the One who knows the way?

Lesson #2:
Obedience Unlocks Favor

If you love Me, you will keep My commands.
—John 14:15 (HCSB)

I quickly learned that obedience unlocks the favor of God. It often serves as an investment into seeing the heavens open in your favor. I made sure to do things in order before the Lord, honoring Him and my spiritual leaders before I made any decisions or moves. Quickly thereafter, the Lord opened up the doors for a space for us to congregate at no cost as we started up a new church. This would be a shared space, but we were ever so grateful nonetheless.

God moved the hearts of even strangers to bless us financially and even performed a miracle: all of our paperwork for the church was approved through the state within weeks even though the process should have taken months. Within six months, we quickly outgrew the space, just as the Lord said would happen, and God opened yet another door. We moved into our own space, and once again, God provided absolutely everything that we needed! This time around, God was not only teaching me the power of faith the size of a mustard seed, but also the entire church. They, too, were beginning to experience the power of moving in obedience.

See, favor has the power to make a way where there seems to be none. Sadly, this also opens the door to much jealousy and envy at times. Let's face it; favor is not fair! And yet that is exactly what makes it so magnificent! We cannot earn it, we cannot buy it, and we cannot manipulate it for it is freely given by a sovereign God. Who are we to dictate how He chooses to bestow it among His children?

There is something about walking in the Lord's favor that makes you feel untouchable. Though we are not invincible, we walk under the protection of the Father, and that in turn makes the enemy want to flee at the very sight of those favored by the Lord. Favor is readily available to every believer so long as they move in obedience, and yet it is so seldomly taken advantage of because of the mere disobedience that many would rather walk in. It is mind-boggling. We must consider obedience as the key that opens the many locked doors before us. There is no secret formula, no trick question, not even a test to ace but rather a simple decision to make: to walk in obedience and in turn see the hand of God.

It all comes down to this simple truth—if we love Him, then we will keep His commands, as the passage above reads. This means that there is a direct correlation between my love for Him and my obedience to Him. In fact, it would be safe to say that my love for God could be measured by my obedience to Him. A person cannot proclaim to be a son or daughter if they do not heed His teachings. This in no way means that we are expected to be perfect, nor does it mean that we are saved by our works, but rather that we comprehend we must live a life that is not contrary to the Scriptures that we claim to live by.

Personally, I will never grow weary of testifying about God's faithfulness! Our church is living proof that there is a direct correlation between walking in obedience and experiencing the favor and power of God! Whether or not one chooses to obey the Lord will depend greatly upon their prayer life. In fact, our decision to either obey or disobey reveals the love or lack of love that we have in our hearts toward our Savior. Obedience is imperative, not only when it seems profitable to you but also when it seems to bring about a loss. We must trust that God will always honor obedience. Before you can walk in favor, you must travel the valley of obedience daily. It is not a one-time deal either, but rather a conscious decision to wake up each day and choose Jesus! It is to choose to carry your cross with honor and deny yourself. It is to abandon your own will for His.

Lesson #3:
Move With or Without Support

But seek first the kingdom of God and His righteousness, and all these things shall be added to you.
—Matthew 6:33 (HCSB)

Unity is such a beautiful thing! It pleases God when His people come together in one accord to do His will. After all, we are one body; we have different functions, different roles, and different titles and positions perhaps, yet we are one body who makes up the bride of Christ. This should be the case, anyway.

It's interesting that Scripture never shows us an occasion where the enemy has been divided against itself, and yet it's the sad state that we often encounter with some of those who claim to be a part of the church of Jesus Christ. The Scriptures teach us that we are so much stronger together. It goes on to discuss the power that exists and manifests when two come into agreement about any matter here on Earth (Matthew 18:19).

The hard truth is that whether you experience an overwhelmingly positive response and support from other believers or if you experience rejection and pushback, your responsibility remains the same before the Lord. You must move on with or without the support! You see, a lack of support will never be a valid excuse before our Father. In fact, it is all the more reason for you to fully submerge yourself into the call of God!

My journey has taught me some difficult lessons along the way. And yet I wouldn't trade them for the world because they have shaped me into who I am becoming today. In addition, they have taught me some of the most valuable things, such as God's faithfulness and provision. I remember telling the Lord I did not want to make any move outside of His will and that if He wouldn't go with me, I would refuse to move. The fact of the matter is that as long as God goes, it does not matter who does not.

The Scriptures instruct us to seek His Kingdom and righteousness first. The goal here is for us as believers to trust in the provision of God. It is not His will that we would live a life of constant worry for our every need. He is calling us to trust in Him completely and to experience how He is our provider. This could be difficult when times are hard, such as facing moments of loneliness or even struggles with finances. We have all been there at one point or another. The Lord is so gracious that He gives us a different approach to take. He tells us to pursue His Kingdom and righteousness first and to trust that He will take care of the rest. So how do we seek this? We live according to His principles, we serve wholeheartedly, and we walk in all that He has called us to.

When we seek His Kingdom and righteousness first, He truly takes care of the rest. I recall on one occasion, the Lord spoke to me and said for me to occupy myself in His things and He would take care of mine. This was a difficult task for me personally as it meant letting go of all control. Ironically, I wanted to control things in my life that I couldn't even begin to handle. In essence, God was doing me a favor by taking a burden off my hands that He never intended for me to carry. Once I realized the absolute peace that there is in handing over all control to Him and focusing on what He called me to do, it became easier and easier to surrender every single area of my life into His hands. Little by little, I have come to encounter the provision that He promises in return for putting Him first.

Lesson #4:
You Are Responsible to Fulfill the Vision

For we are His creation, created in Christ Jesus for good works, which God prepared ahead of time so that we should walk in them.
—Ephesians 2:10 (HCSB)

We all have been created with a purpose. The Scriptures are clear that God has prepared these things ahead of time so that we may walk in them. This means that before we were even conceived, God already had a plan. He had a plan before and after people had an opinion. He had a plan before and after you committed many mistakes. He had a plan before and after everyone walked away and left you to face the reality of life all on your own. See, God's plans never have been and never will be dependent upon others. It has always been centered on you.

It is important to note that the good works mentioned in this Scripture are not a basis for salvation. We are not saved by our works but by grace alone. However, they are the very evidence of a life transformed in Christ. Furthermore, it is imperative that we understand that these good works are not a mere suggestion or request on behalf of the Lord but rather a command and expectation. We are the only beings that come into existence with a life already perfectly orchestrated by an omniscient God, if only we choose to allow Him to lead.

And yet in His just nature, He allows us to choose whom we will serve.

This means that the vision has already been established, and we have been given the responsibility and the privilege to fulfill it. I love the fact that God has no need to operate using backup plans or strategies. His thoughts and ways are always higher. The beauty of it is that He would never give us a vision that we would not be able to fulfill along with Him. The issue lies with our trouble to believe that. We so frequently develop an unhealthy dependence on others that we shift our focus off of the very One who has called us. But what happens when those against you seem to be greater in number than those who support you?

This is a valley that I have traveled on more occasions than I would like to remember. Yet if there is one thing that God has always made clear to me throughout, it is that I have been given the responsibility to fulfill the vision despite it all! Understand, when you set out to fulfill a vision placed in your heart by the Lord, it appears that hell itself rises up against you in diverse ways. Most often, these attacks come in a form of intimidation. The goal is to make you fear and cease your labors. You must comprehend that the enemy of our souls often knows the plan over your life better than you do. He has no end to his schemes in an attempt to bring you to your demise.

Pursuing the vision of God alone is one of the absolute hardest things I have ever endured. People always say they'll be there for you, but when it is time for you to hit the ground running and begin to pay the price of the calling, they are conspicuously absent. You will find that you are most often met with criticism rather than offers to assist. After all, anyone can do the job better when they are not in your shoes. I will not pretend that fulfilling the vision of the Lord is an easy task. But if it were easy, perhaps it would not be worth it. I have learned that people will come and go, but the vision must go on.

Lesson #5:
Present Doesn't Always Mean Present

Then He said to His disciples, "The harvest is abundant, but the workers are few."
—Matthew 9:37 (HCSB)

Just because people are there does not mean they are there for the right reasons. Over the years of servitude, I have experienced a lot. I have seen and heard so many prophecies spoken over fellow brethren, and yet rarely have I had the opportunity to see them come to fruition. I have often asked myself a recurring question: Why? The truth of the matter is that God does not change. In fact, the Scriptures teach us that His Spirit is always willing (Matthew 26:41). This proves that the issue is not Him but rather us.

In Matthew 9, we see a wide array of miracles and works that Jesus performed. We read about Him healing a paralytic man, calling Matthew as a disciple, sitting with sinners, healing a woman with an issue of blood, raising a young girl back to life, healing not one but two blind men, and let us not forget healing a man who was unable to speak. This list is exhausting to even think about, and then we take into account that while He was doing all of these things, He was also under the microscope of the Pharisees, who were constantly scrutinizing His every move.

Is it not interesting that there never seems to be a lack of that pharisaical spirit lingering around? No matter how well Jesus did, they found a way to criticize Him all the more. Why do we expect anything less? Most often, the ones who have so much to say are the ones who do the least. When you are assignment driven, you understand that you have no time to criticize how everyone else does things because you have a job to do.

Jesus then ends the chapter by expressing to His disciples that the harvest is abundant but the workers are few (Matthew 9:37). We must understand that in His earthly existence, He was susceptible to all the things that we face, such as growing tired physically, becoming hungry, and feeling physical limitations. However, He was making a point that we live in a world that needs salvation. The people are the harvest! There is no shortage of those who need the Kingdom of the Gospel to be proclaimed to them. What we have a shortage of are workers willing to put in the work.

The Pharisees were present, the Scribes were present, and even some disciples were already present, and yet none helped to lessen the load on Jesus. Now, we know that He was fully capable, but this also mirrors the condition of many in our churches today. Growth in numbers means absolutely nothing if people are not willing to help bear the weight of the mission, unite with the vision, and walk in the call.

One of my constant prayers to the Lord is for Him to send us people who want to work for His Kingdom! We can teach them, we can equip them, we can guide them, but at the end of it all, they have to be willing to apply it all. Never pray for quantity but quality! I have learned that we could accomplish so much more for the Kingdom of God with a few dedicated servants than with a multitude of people who have all the knowledge but zero passion. This call requires a love for the souls! Moreover, that love has to often be sacrificial as well. We can choose to be a part of the problem or the solution.

Lesson #6:
The Leech Syndrome

Don't be deceived: God is not mocked. For whatever a man sows he will also reap, because the one who sows to his flesh will reap corruption from the flesh, but the one who sows to the Spirit will reap eternal life from the Spirit.
—*Galatians 6:7–8 (HCSB)*

There is something that we must thoroughly comprehend, and that is that the anointing attracts! The anointing that God places over your life has a way of drawing people in. This, at times, can be a great blessing and a tool to use in evangelism. However, it is not without its disadvantages. Many people will flock to you for the wrong reasons as well. With time, God always reveals the motives and exposes the intentions of their heart, but if you are not careful, they could wreak havoc. This is why discernment is key.

A leech is a wormlike creature with suckers on both sides. They are bloodsucking parasites. As if that were not bad enough, they not only extract from their victims but are pretty generous in leaving behind unwanted gifts. This is because they are also carriers of viruses and bacteria and often pass these along to their unsuspecting victims. Most interestingly, though, is the reason that they operate the way they do. You see, leeches need blood in order to survive. In fact, they need blood in order to grow and reproduce.

Now, in case you are not following me yet, allow me to explain. Within those who call themselves part of the body of Christ, you will find something that the Lord shared with me called the Leech Syndrome. This is a condition that some people carry—in a spiritual sense, of course—that makes them use and abuse the people of God in their lives. These people are master manipulators and deceivers, and they excel in making you believe that they are in unity with you and your vision, that they have been sent to help with the mission, that they honor and respect your mantle, and that they appreciate what they can learn from you, but the reality is that they come with a hidden agenda.

The hidden agenda could consist of many factors and variables; however, it is always evil and demonic in nature. Their primary goal here is not to bring glory and honor to God but rather to self. Especially in much of the generation that we are witnessing rise up today, there is such a hunger for fame, recognition, and status. The value of work ethic is slowly dying out, the need to be processed through trials seems to be a thing of the past, and sacrifice is no longer a prerequisite. Many are being bottle-fed a watered-down Gospel that focuses more on the achievements and accolades than humility and servitude. Then we wonder why the church seems to have strayed so far from the Great Commission given to us by Jesus.

Dealing with a carrier of this syndrome is extremely mentally exhausting, but the most devastating part is that you often do not know right away. The enemy has a way of hiding his claws until you least expect it. This is why we must be constantly connected to our Source in prayer, not only because of how draining and toxic these situations have the potential to become but also because of the effects that they leave on you as a person and your ministry. Many people are often affected by these unfortunate events, and sadly, many even fall to the wayside under the demonic influence of said believers.

The Leech Syndrome sows to the flesh; after all, it creates a self-focused mentality, and those who practice it will reap corruption from the flesh. I believe that some people very mistakenly believe that they will escape judgment because we serve a God who abounds in mercy. This is precisely the point that Paul was making to the Galatians. The love of God is real, as are His mercy and grace, but these do not negate the consequences of our actions. When we falsely believe and even convince ourselves that we will get away scot-free from the consequences of our sin, we are essentially trying to mock God. Paul made it clear to the Galatians, as I want to make it clear to you, that a man will always reap what he has sown. Be sure to sow in the Spirit as this will allow us to reap eternal life from the Spirit.

Lesson #7:
Nip It in the Bud

If your brother sins against you, go and rebuke him in private. If he listens to you, you have won your brother.
—Matthew 18:15 (HCSB)

If you are anything like me, you hate conflict. Regrettably, conflict in your walk with Christ is inevitable. Sooner or later, you will find yourself in the midst of an issue, whether you are the cause, a victim, or simply a witness. I have learned over time that the longer you allow conflict to persist, grow, or remain unattended, the more damage it has the potential to cause. The reason for this is due to who is behind it all. We must understand that conflict comes for one reason and one reason only: to create division. And who exactly is behind division? The enemy of our soul himself: Satan.

In this portion of Scripture, Jesus was teaching His disciples the process of dealing with sin-related conflict within a group of believers. His instructions are very simple but often complicated by us. He instructed them to rebuke a person in private, and if that did not work, there are step-by-step instructions on how to proceed. In this day and age, these private sessions are not often heard of. With the advancement of technology, face-to-face communication has diminished greatly. Lamentably, many have shied away from resolving conflict altogether, let alone in a way that honors God. What we do see more and more commonly is the use of things such as social media, gossip, and character assassination in place of simply talking to our brethren. It appears that it has become easier to talk *about* people rather than talk *to* people.

It is imperative that we go about this with the foreknowledge that the goal here is restoration. When you confront your brother or sister, the objective should not be to determine the initial fault. In fact, at times the miniscule details are actually irrelevant. Discussing these things could potentially lead to worsening the problem rather than resolving it. The purpose of such a meeting is to win your brother or sister over. Communication is key in every type of relationship. There are times that we offend one another, and it is completely unintentional; sometimes, we are not even aware until it is brought to our attention. And when this happens, the correct thing to do is acknowledge our brethren's feelings and genuinely apologize. Allow me to add that apologizing does not make us less of a Christian or less holy. On the contrary, it reveals that we comprehend that we, too, fail and that we need a Savior as we are not perfect.

One of the best things that one can do is to nip conflict in the bud. To nip something in the bud is to put a quick end to something or shut it down at an early stage. This is important because in doing so, you are putting a limit on the damage that it could cause. When you go through the channels to resolve conflict quickly, you are no longer giving a foothold to the enemy. As previously mentioned, conflict is always going to present itself along the way, no matter how careful you are, but it is not so much the conflict that defines you but how you handle it.

I have had my fair share of conflicts to resolve along the way, some of which ended peacefully and others that, unfortunately, I have had no control over. If there is one thing that I have learned in terms of conflict, it is that the final result is not determined by you alone. There is a mutual agreement that has to take place. Both parties must be on the same page with the same goal in order for it to end amicably. However, in times where the other party simply refuses or decides to profusely attack and persist in their behaviors, then be at peace knowing that you have done your part to the best of your ability. In verse 17, Jesus instructed the disciples that if, after all was said and done, the person still pays no attention, let him be like an unbeliever. Just be cautious to guard your heart from any resentment or indifference. The easiest way to do this is to show them the genuine love of Christ when you see them and pray for abundant blessing over their lives.

Lesson #8:
Be Gracefully Firm

I have written you this brief letter through Silvanus (I know him to be a faithful brother) to encourage you and to testify that this is the true grace of God. Take your stand in it!
—1 Peter 5:12 (HCSB)

At times, being graceful and being firm appear to be total opposites of each other. Despite this, they actually go hand in hand. The Scriptures teach us the importance of operating in grace and standing firm in it. However, when we are instructed to stand firm in something, it means that there will come a time where pressure will be applied for us to sway from what we stand on—hence the importance of standing firm on grace.

The letter written in 1 Peter is one of exhortation to the people of God. Its purpose is to teach them how to be holy and to emulate the suffering of Jesus. Peter expounds on this topic with the people through Silvanus, a faithful brother. The church was experiencing persecution, and Peter saw it fit to encourage them and remind them that the Gospel of Jesus is the true grace and that it was imperative that they stood firm in it.

Today, there are so many things that draw us away from God. Many are facing temptations that they didn't even know they secretly desired in the most intimate part of their hearts. There are pressures from everywhere that make it seem much easier to simply let go and completely walk away from God. The truth is that in our human nature, we are all guilty of sin and rebellion against God. What we have earned is eternal condemnation. However, due to the Father sending Jesus to give His life at Calvary on our behalf, we have been saved by grace. Peter is exhorting us all to stand in such grace. In order to do this, we must turn away from our sinful rebellion.

So what does this look like exactly in our walk? At times, it will look like you are a loner, standing firm on principles that others have compromised. Other times, it will look like you are the antagonist simply because you want to guard your heart and your walk. There will be moments where you will be accused of thinking you are too good for everyone else simply because you refuse to trade the truth for the temporary carnal pleasures of this world. The reality is that everyone will always have an opinion on your walk, your life, and your choices, but you must stand firm on God's grace in spite of them.

If there is one thing that I have learned about being graceful, it is that oftentimes people see it as a sign of weakness. Grace, however, is nowhere near weakness. People will, at times, want to push over you and take advantage of your gracefulness because they perceive it to be frailty in your decisions. When they do not agree with what you do or say, they will attempt to find ways to overcome it, even at times distorting the Word to their own advantage.

Have you ever been caught in the middle of a sudden storm? The rain begins to pummel you no matter how fast you run. The hurricane-like winds seem as if they could just sweep you right off your feet into the air. Or you might imagine yourself at the beach, where even the calm sea finds a way to forcefully push you as you simply stand by the edge of the water. The pressures of life have this same effect at times. You try to stand firm, but this does not stop the threat to your stance.

In the midst of these things, we are still instructed to stand firm in grace. Standing firm does not mean to be cruel, but showing grace does not mean to be a pushover either. Grace and standing firm, in actuality, balance each other out evenly. The grace of God is freely given, and none of us are worthy of it. We must stand firm on it—not our truth, as many today would call it to support their own lustful desires—but the truth of God. The truth of God does not change. The Gospel of Jesus is the grace of God, so stand firm in it.

Lesson #9:
Show Grace

Indeed, we have all received grace after grace from His fullness.
—John 1:16 (HCSB)

Grace is such a precious gift. It is a pure joy to experience the unmerited favor of our Lord and Savior. Perhaps more than anything it is because we know that we are so unworthy of it. Have you ever failed God miserably in such a manner that you would totally understand if He refused to ever deal with you again? Those are the precise moments when His grace shines the most! We are deserving of His vengeance and wrath, but we receive His unconditional love, mercy, and grace instead.

John explains to us that we are privileged to receive grace upon grace only because Jesus is full of said grace. Nevertheless, grace can often be a bit difficult to practice with others. We are taught that we must work hard for the things that we want to achieve, but grace operates under a different principle. It then puts us in position to show grace to others despite them having done nothing to receive it. After all, we are to give by grace what we have received by grace.

As humans, we are limited in our perspectives of each and every situation that we encounter. We have a tendency to want to focus on fairness. In fact, our moral compass could even make us naturally defensive when we feel that someone is not deserving of grace. And yet that is the very idea encapsulated by grace, that it is not something that you could earn. Oftentimes, we get so wrapped up in the difficulty of displaying such grace with others that we begin to take a legalistic approach. If this is where you are, allow me to give you a tip: God's grace can never be fully understood.

I thought I had mastered, to some extent at least, the idea of showing people grace. That was until I realized that in pastoring, you are introduced to an entirely different level of requirement of grace. I like to think of grace having different levels. It is the best way that I can explain it. These are not levels that you want to achieve voluntarily but levels that God introduces you to as you mature spiritually and meet new people. New people bring along new problems, new situations, new trials, and new hurdles. I found myself having to forgive over and over and over again. At times, I experienced offenses that were, without a doubt, intentional, others that were pure negligence, and some that were genuine mistakes. It has forced me to gain a deeper understanding that, even as Christians, we mess up.

Though this is a lifelong journey and lesson, I have definitely learned some tricks along the way that have aided me in showing grace to others. For starters, I constantly remind myself of how many times God has shown me grace, all the times that He simply should have given up and ran far away from me and instead His love drew me in closer. Reminding myself of how many times I have experienced the grace of God helps me to be more considerate and compassionate toward others. Another thing that has helped me to show grace is to ask myself how I would want to be treated. This method helps me to take a breather and sincerely analyze the situation before responding. Once we acknowledge that we all fall short of His glory, we will be more likely to show grace to one another and set the example of Jesus.

Lesson #10:
I'm Not Your Competition

Whatever you do, do it enthusiastically, as something done for the Lord and not for men.
—*Colossians 3:23 (HCSB)*

I know what you are thinking—there is no place for competition in the church. That should be the case. I wish that were the case. I hate to be the bearer of bad news, but it certainly exists within the body. It baffles me, in all honesty, that the goal of some would be to defeat each other rather than our mutual enemy, the ruler of darkness. The constant drive for ministers to prove themselves better than the next minister further exposes the sad truth of their hearts. It begs the question: What is your true intention?

A competitive mindset can become so destructive, both for the one competing and the one they compete against. It establishes the idea that the objective is to establish superiority over another. This is an extremely dangerous mindset because the Scripture is clear that God does not share His glory. As the church of Jesus Christ, we should strive to unify our efforts in advancing the Kingdom of Heaven here on Earth. After all, we should be on the same mission.

Regardless of your calling, position, or role, we are called to honor God with all that we do.

Sadly, we have entered an era of "who can do it better?" It has become about who coordinates and executes the greatest events, revivals, services, and concerts. Another priority has become the attendance numbers and promotions. In fact, it gets worse. We are witnessing a full-on battle about who preaches best, who sings better, and who can prophesy the most. There is no longer a spirit of compassion and regard for one another but rather one-upmanship.

I have battled with this particular lesson for quite some time now. In total transparency, this battle became present before I even officially began to pastor a church. Having been in evangelistic ministry for about five years prior to pastoring, I had the privilege to visit many churches near and far and had the opportunity to work in leadership for years within the local church I was a member of. My heart has always been set on serving, no matter what that looked like. I was never, nor will I ever be, after a title. How I desire to be able to say the same about everyone that I have encountered, but that would be far from the truth.

I have learned over time that despite your commitment to doing things wholeheartedly for the Lord, there will always be people that your actions do not sit well with. Furthermore, I have learned that instead of some brethren rejoicing when God begins to work through you and use you, they actually become bothered. You see, when a leader is insecure in their position, you will always appear as a threat to them. In spite of you having absolutely no interest in usurping their role, their lens of insufficiency blinds them from seeing you as the blessing that you are in their life.

Paul was expressing to the Colossians that, when you treat all that you do as if it were for the Lord, your heart will always have the correct posture. One of the greatest ways that I have discovered to guard myself from this spirit of competition is to nurture a servant's heart within myself, remembering that I am not worthy of any credit or glory, for without Him I am nothing more than a willing vessel. I made a commitment to God and myself that the moment that I began to make ministry about me, I would remove myself completely because to continue in that condition would be a disservice to those under my leadership.

Lesson #11:
You Cannot Want It More than Them

But if it doesn't please you to worship Yahweh, choose for yourselves today the one you will worship: the gods your fathers worshiped beyond the Euphrates River or the gods of the Amorites in whose land you are living. As for me and my family, we will worship Yahweh.
—Joshua 24:15 (HCSB)

As a Pastor, one of your greatest joys is seeing people not only come to Christ, but grow and develop into everything that God has spoken over their lives. This, however, can also be a double-edged sword. That is because this only works if the person is willing to pay the price, to put in the work and sacrifice. When you see someone completely throw away all that God has put in their hands, it becomes difficult to not take it personally. A shepherd's heart, after all, desires to protect and guide the flock.

Have you ever had moments where you just wanted to shake someone and wake them up from their spiritual slumber? Because you will have many of those in ministry. One of the hardest lessons that I have had to come to terms with is that I cannot want it more than them. I cannot want the passion, the growth, or the fire of God more than them. You see, you can equip people with all the tools, give them the best training, and even accompany them for support, but at the end of it all, they still have to perform the duty themselves.

In the Scripture above, we find Joshua, who was nearing the end of his journey. He had gathered the people of Israel to speak to them on behalf of the Lord. Joshua recounts what they have been through with the intention of shining light on the need for them to be committed in their walk to the One true God. He confronts them for their split devotions. Many of them were still secretly worshiping idols, and God was demanding a total commitment to Him. Joshua declares that he and his house would serve the Lord and tells the rest of them to choose today whom they would serve.

This is the very same scenario that we run into today. We are surrounded by people who have not only seen but experienced the faithfulness of God. We are surrounded by people who have tasted His goodness. We are surrounded by people who, over and over again, have seen how God fights for His children. And yet we still are surrounded by people who appear one way externally but secretly worship other idols internally. Their hearts are not fully yielded before the Lord because they refuse to let go of the very things that hinder their walk.

See, our hearts are exposed by what we do. Our failure to walk in what God has called us to do exposes the lack of relationship in our heart. Unfortunately, you cannot obligate someone to be passionate about the Lord. When you know God, you love Him. When you love God, you obey Him. When you obey God, you walk in His will. It is very simple. This is not a matter of whether I want to follow the will of the Lord, but rather will I do it? It is a choice, a choice that every individual person must make on their own accord, and that is where this becomes very challenging for those in leadership. It is our utmost desire to see a person excel in what the Lord has spoken, but what happens when they do not?

I still remember how the Lord responded to me one day as I prayed about this very issue. He said to me, "Do not beg them to serve Me!" I was a bit astonished as I had always felt that part of my job was to give that extra boost when needed. Through much prayer, however, I was able to understand exactly what the Lord meant. He is not interested in people doing His will with an indifferent attitude, for misery has no place in the Gospel. God wants us to serve Him because we want to, not because someone else wants us to. He wants us to understand the privilege it is to not only serve Him, but to work in His Kingdom. In order for us to walk in the fullness of our relationship with the Lord, we must choose whom we will serve as we cannot serve two masters.

Lesson #12:
Lonely Stroll

Turn to me and be gracious to me, for I am alone and afflicted.
—Psalm 25:16 (HCSB)

Imagine being surrounded by so many people and still feeling lonely. Could we just be completely honest for a moment? Ministry is lonely! I am always taken aback when I see people aspiring for large ministries. Perhaps they truly have no idea what they are asking for. A renowned ministry is not the objective here. It is not a place that you reach, nor a level that you attain and celebrate as some sort of accomplishment. As a matter of fact, ministry is to serve. Jesus Himself expressed to His disciples that He did not come to be served but to serve (Matthew 20:28).

The psalmist knew the feeling of loneliness all too well. At the particular time when this psalm was written, his sons and friends had turned their backs on him. David was feeling abandoned. Yet he knew that there was One who would not leave him nor forsake him. Though he was no stranger to the desperation that loneliness brings about on a person, it did not lessen the impact. Perhaps he was taken back to the moments that he spent alone shepherding his father's flock. Perhaps he was thinking about all the times that God had come through for Him. And yet in this moment, there seemed to be silence. Have you ever experienced a time that felt like the absence of God? For the psalmist to ask the Lord to turn to him implied that he believed that the Lord had turned from him at some point. Talk about a moment of desperation.

There are moments where the silence of God can be so deafening in our lives, where we go through things that we simply cannot comprehend. And as if His silence were not enough, it feels amplified by the solitude that you feel when around the body of Christ. How could it be that the very ones meant to lift up your hands in your moments of despair are often absent? This is a question that everyone in ministry will ask at some point. Things worsen when that feeling of hopelessness gets coupled with the attacks of the enemy on your mind that begin to tell you that nobody cares or even notices what you are going through.

You desperately want someone to embrace you and assure you that everything will be all right. Then you remember that you are that person, the one everyone depends on, counts on, looks to for a word of encouragement, and who inspires faith in others. If you're not careful, this has the potential to become a weapon of mass destruction to your own heart. It is at this moment you must realize that the One you run to is God. He is your strength. He is your refuge. He is your peace.

As much as you desire for people to fully understand what you feel, think, or perhaps even fear, you cannot expect this from someone outside of your shoes. Other ministers may relate, but nobody outside of our Lord will ever fully comprehend the intricacies of what you feel and face. Though your pillow may hold many secrets, your notebooks are filled with the thoughts that bombard your mind, and your tears are simply flushed down the drain, none of these can ever replace the feeling of releasing it all to the Lord in prayer.

Ministry is often a lonely stroll. You will cross many valleys that you wish to never visit again. The reality is that you very well may have to. As you encounter diverse people in different walks of life, you will begin to understand why God has allowed many of those valleys in your own life. Your testimony has so much more credibility and impact when you have actually been through some things. However, you must remember that not even the loneliest, darkest, and coldest moments can scare God's presence away. He is there for it all. He is by your side simply waiting for you to call on Him. We must trust Him, even through the silence.

Lesson #13:
Do Not Take It Personally

Don't pay attention to everything people say, or you may hear your servant cursing you, for you know that many times you yourself have cursed others.
—Ecclesiastes 7:21–22 (HCSB)

We live in a world that seeks to be offended. I know that is a hard truth to swallow, but it is still true nonetheless. We have become supersensitive to so many things. In fact, we have even found ways to take things personally that, at times, are none of our concern. Ministry is not the place for this. You will learn rather quickly the need for a thick skin. This can be difficult to achieve but not impossible. It requires you to defeat defensiveness, to love like Christ, and to release your sense of entitlement.

This applies to both the things done unintentionally and those intentional attacks against your character, your testimony, and your person. The Scriptures teach us that none of us are perfect. This makes us all susceptible to moments of weakness when we have the potential to slip up. The truth is that we have all said some things that we have regretted afterward. In other words, we have been on both sides of the fence with this. At times, you may have been the victim, and at others, you may have been the aggressor.

Isn't it interesting, though, how the negative things said about you always find a way to your ears? As much as you want to avoid it and guard your heart, somehow, someway, we always find out the things that were spoken about us in a destructive manner. The enemy sees to it that a seed of hate, rejection, and revenge is planted one way or another. And yet at times, we are our own culprit when we go seeking the information ourselves. One of the worst things that you can do is to go digging for the things said about you. This leads you to closely examine every word, and from examining each word, you begin rehearsing them in your mind. This eventually leads to a heart that will meditate on revenge. Allow me to share with you that the Holy Spirit will never lead you to seek revenge against anyone. The Lord is clear that vengeance is His (Deuteronomy 32:35).

We must not forget that ministry is all about dealing with people. Every person comes dragging their own burdens, facing their own trials, and being tormented by their own demons. The church is to be a hospital where people come to be made well. Jesus Himself said that the sick are the ones who need a doctor (Luke 5:31–32). This needs to be the primary focus when working with the souls. We need to meet them where they are and restore them, not forgetting where we once were. There simply is no time for offense.

This can be so difficult when you feel like you are personally under attack. I have run into this dilemma over and over again throughout the years. Learning the art of silence is probably one of the hardest lessons that a minister could learn and one of the most powerful. The reward is always sure to follow. God is our defender. Trust me; it hurts—it hurts badly when you have to sit in silence and watch while the very ones you have served try to destroy your name. But I have seen God fight for me over and over again. This is a guarantee for those who remain silent and wait on the Lord, for He is a just God.

As servants, we must also let go of a sense of entitlement. The truth is we are not owed absolutely anything. Defeating defensiveness begins with understanding that nobody owes you a thing. We must rid ourselves of wanting to constantly defend every aspect of our lives.

When you understand that not everything requires an explanation, you are fully able to move past things and continue to move forward. Overall, learning to love like Christ is the pivotal point here. To love like Christ is to look past the rough exterior, the flaws, the mistakes, the offenses, and to look to the heart. It is to see someone as God sees them. It becomes very hard to hate someone or harbor anger against someone when you look at them as God does.

Lesson #14:
To Invest or to Divest

Do not be deceived: "Bad company corrupts good morals."
—*1 Corinthians 15:33 (HCSB)*

Ever since I came to Christ, I have heard of the importance of pouring into others. We have the responsibility to share the Gospel and to love like Jesus. This has always led me to consider the beauty of investing in others. Whether that investment consists of time, teaching, finances, guidance or anything of that nature, I have always understood it to be a blessing. After all, I would not be where I am today if others had not taken the time to invest and pour into my life as well.

We must get a full understanding of the context of this Scripture. Paul was writing to the Corinthians regarding false teachers who had come in teaching that the resurrection of Jesus was false. In fact, they did not believe in life after death, and this is what they were teaching the people. It is important to not be misled. False teachings and ungodly relationships will never lead us to inherit the Kingdom of God, nor will adopting corrupt lifestyles ever lead us to holiness. Regardless of how firm you believe you are, over time, even the strongest Christians tend to waver in their faith under submission to corruption. Influence has a power that can be either good or bad, and you often can't recognize it until you are in full submission to it.

The unfortunate truth is that not everyone who shows up to church is there for God. Not everyone that calls themselves a Christian is really a Christian. Just because they claim to be a part of the body does not make them entitled to attach themselves to you. Discernment is absolutely necessary, especially in this day and age. You will find that it is not only important to know when to invest in someone but also when to divest. Both functions are necessary, and both must be put to practice in ministry.

"To divest" can be defined as depriving someone of something. To be more specific, when you divest yourself of something, it is to no longer be responsible for it. I know that this may sound a bit contradictory with the Gospel; however, it is crucial to recognize where you are to apply your time and resources, lest you find yourself exhausting your resources on people who have no interest in growing and denying those who do desire growth the support to do so. This is why not just anyone can be under your leadership.

Learning to differentiate between who to invest in and who to divest from can be difficult at times. Over the years, I have found myself on both sides of this issue. I have had the privilege to pour into many and to see the growth of those same people in their walk with the Lord. But I have also seen the error of my ways at times when I continued to pour into people who I should have divested from long ago. Now, by no means am I saying that they should not be around. The people that you divest from could still stick around, but your focus cannot be primarily on them.

Your time is invaluable. Time is something that you can never get back, hence the importance of using our time wisely. The same could be said about our resources and investments. Though pouring into people who simply have no genuine interest should never be considered a waste—after all, your hope is that you have planted a seed—it often comes at the expense of those who have a true hunger for the Lord. Be cautious to never deprive those who thirst for the Gospel.

This becomes clearer through constant prayer. Do not be so quick to take on people to mentor or even take people under your leadership for the sake of numbers. Doing this can leave you completely drained with absolutely nothing to show for it. Rather, allow the Lord to lead your every move and every decision, for He will never lead you astray.

Lesson #15:
A Woman Pastor

"For My thoughts are not your thoughts, and your ways are not My ways." This is the Lord's declaration.
—Isaiah 55:8 (HCSB)

For starters, let's make something clear. I did *not* ask for this! I don't know who in their right mind would ask for such a responsibility from the Lord. Shepherding the people of God in a time of such corruption in our world is hard even with all the support possible. Now, add to that the simple fact that a woman Pastor is not accepted by some, ridiculed by others, and downright disrespected in many cases. It truly requires you to know the God who has called you and to walk in total dependence on and obedience to Him. For the record, in spite of all of the difficulties that come with the territory, I would not trade it for the world. Walking in total obedience to the Lord, despite what that may look like at times, has been such an incredible and rewarding journey for me.

One of the primary things that I have had to learn to do is to resist the temptation of wanting to explain myself to people who do not agree with the office that God has called me to. I have learned that some people will ask questions with no intent of listening to the answer. At times, these discussions lead to disagreements and in no way provide any type of edification for anyone involved. It is important to understand the why behind what you do and, even more importantly, who you do it for. Your focus must remain on the God that called you and the people that you serve.

A woman Pastor is such a widely debated topic that some prefer to not discuss it at all. This may explain why women Pastors in lead roles make up only about 10 percent of the churches across America. As if these hurdles were not enough, in my case, singleness was also a factor. I will never forget some of the comments that I received when I first began to speak about what God was calling me to do, nor will I ever forget some of the looks of disbelief. After all, this is a man's place, not a woman's, according to many.

We serve a sovereign God. This means that He is a supreme ruler and does things however He sees fit. The bottom line is that our Father is not looking for a particular gender, age, or size but rather a willing heart. This is precisely why He told the prophet Samuel that David was a man after His own heart (1 Samuel 13:14). God is seeking a willing generation to arise and to be His hands and feet here on Earth. Sadly, many have fallen away from what God has called them to do, but where there is a willing vessel, God will use it for His glory.

The Bible endorses women in leadership. Paul's first letter to Timothy seems to limit women's roles in leadership (1 Timothy 2:12), yet that idea comes in direct contrast to other passages where Paul also praised the women who served with him as co-laborers—women such as Phoebe (Romans 16:1–2), Junia (Romans 16:7), and Priscilla, who helped lay the foundation of the early church (1 Corinthians 16:19). There are other women like Deborah, a judge and prophet, and the Samaritan woman who became the first evangelist. Paul refers to other women who led churches, such as Chloe (1 Corinthians 1:11) and Nympha (Colossians 4:15), and he never tried to hinder, silence, or restrict them. Those who are against women in leadership positions also always refer to 1 Timothy 2:12, but they ignore the women who served with Paul.

People often like to use 1 Corinthians 14:34–35 in regard to women being silent in the church, showing it as biblical proof that women cannot be Pastors. Though it is a passage on bringing order within the church meetings, it cannot be taken out of context. Paul was addressing the condition of the church and saw the need to silence the disruptive speech. Their worship was chaotic, and he wanted to bring order. It wasn't only the women that he addressed but also the prophets. It does not mean that a woman cannot speak. It is also important to note that this idea came from Roman law, not Jewish law. The Romans did not see women as equals, and therefore they also were not permitted to hold any type of political office, power, or authority. The Jewish law did not forbid women to speak, not even in public gatherings.

Paul encouraged faithful women. If God calls a woman to Pastor, she is the head of the church, the angel of the church that God has established. The difference is at home, if she is married, in which the man is still the head. The original design still stands. Just in terms of the church, she is the highest authority after God if she is the one with the calling to Pastor. The bottom line is that God is going to use a stone if He has to in order to get His work done. Interestingly enough, I have found that some of the same people who claim to be profusely against a woman being a Pastor would still receive a word from the Lord through them without a second thought. In conclusion, the Bible teaches us that His ways and His thoughts are much higher than our own. We may not always understand why He works the way He does, but it is not our duty to understand but to obey. We are His creation and were created for good works. Therefore, it is imperative that we strive to achieve every assignment that God has laid out for each of us with excellence.

About The Author

I am the lead Pastor of Hope Restored Church and the Founder of Captivating Grace Ministries. I have been Pastoring for two years. We are a bilingual church that loves to serve! I was an Evangelist for about five years prior to becoming a Pastor. I was born and raised in Lancaster, PA. I have two children, a boy and a girl. My daughter Sariah is 16 and my son Zyel is 15. I am also recently engaged. I am fully bilingual in English and Spanish and this has been a great tool and blessing in ministry as I interpret for myself. I have a passion to serve and love to preach, teach, sing and write.

Milton Keynes UK
Ingram Content Group UK Ltd.
UKHW021521011224
451361UK00006B/197